Michael Brennan | Autoethnographic

New Poems

GIRAMONDO POETS

Michael Brennan | Autoethnographic

First published 2012
from the Writing & Society Research Centre
at the University of Western Sydney
by the Giramondo Publishing Company
PO Box 752 Artarmon NSW 1570 Australia
www.giramondopublishing.com

Designed by Harry Williamson
Typeset by Andrew Davies
in 10/16.5 pt Baskerville

Printed and bound by Ligare
Distributed in Australia by NewSouth Books

National Library of Australia
Cataloguing-in-Publication data:

Brennan, Michael, 1973–
Autoethnographic / Michael Brennan
ISBN 978-1-920882-89-1 (pbk.)
A821.3

For Kim Selling & Matt Tripolone

Other books by Michael Brennan

Poetry
The Imageless World
Language Habits
Unanimous Night

Collaborations
空は空／*Sky was sky* (with Akiko Muto and Yasuhiro Yotsumoto)
Atopia (with Kay Orchison)
Asylum (with Yasuhiro Yotsumoto)

As editor
A cool and shaded heart: Collected Poems of Noel Rowe
Calyx: 30 Contemporary Australian Poets (with Peter Minter)
Absence and Negativity

Acknowledgements

Dorothy Porter (ed.), *The Best Australian Poems 2006*; Robert Adamson (ed.) *The Best Australian Poems 2010*; John Kinsella & Ouyang Yu (eds.), *Contemporary Australian Poetry in Chinese Translation* (2007); John Kinsella (ed.), *The Turnrow Anthology of Contemporary Australian Poetry* (2012), *Language habits* (2008); *Asylum* (with Yasuhiro Yotsumoto, 2012); Red Room Company Toilet Doors Project, 2004; Poets Paint Words II, Sydney Writers Festival 2009; *Australian Book Review*, damau.org, *HEAT, Jacket, Jacket2, Rabbit, Salt Magazine, Snorkel, Southerly* and *VLAK*. Especial thanks to Nguyễn Tiên Hoàng, Lưu Diệu Vân and Ouyang Yu and Yasuhiro Yotsumoto for translation and publication of some of these poems in Vietnamese, Chinese and Japanese; heartfelt thanks to Mabel Lee, Tomaž Šalamun and Samuel Wagan Watson, Elizabeth Webby, Kay Orchison, Chris Edwards, Liz Allen, Erico Tonotsuka for the use of her image *Combining*, 2005 on p. viii and to Ivor Indyk & Giramondo.

Human beings do not live in the objective world alone, nor alone in the world of social activity as ordinarily understood, but are very much at the mercy of the particular language which has become the medium of expression for their society. It is quite an illusion to imagine that one adjusts to reality essentially without the use of language and that language is merely an incidental means of solving specific problems of communication and reflection. The fact of the matter is that the 'real world' is to a large extent unconsciously built up on the language habits of the group.

EDWARD SAPIR, *Language*

We look at the world through eyes of ancient mud.

JOHN GRAY, *Straw Dogs*

Contents

Who is Alibi Wednesday?

Don't worry too much, it's all taken care of. That's what the city tells you. You're goo-goo about it, fresh off the boat, looking to be the grit in its dozen oysters. The tide rushes in and out of Sydney Harbour, as though the city was breathing. It's been doing it for years! Only after the pretty blonde from the Welcoming Party checks your papers does she snip the stitches from your lips and pass you a *Southerly Buster*. The smugglers told you the truth: This city squeals delightfully in equal portions of vodka, ice and speed. It's a heady mix, and after your forty days in the desert, you're looking for a bit of fun. You're so happy you shout beautiful curses in a language no one understands. The executioner rolls in, all black mask, bowie knife and speech pathology. When you feel the blade's tongue lick your throat, you are still giddily scratching surfaces, falling in love with the city.

The journey in

On the journey in there was a vestibule, that's what I'd call it, though obviously that's not a word you habituate to without a little effort, but there it was, a vestibule alright, where Emmett Dalgliesh took my coat and hat and gave me a ticket he said I could exchange at the petting zoo for something warm and moist called Mavis. When I looked to the plunge pool, all I saw were endless formations of migratory birds puncturing the sky as they headed this way and that home to roost. The Jackal-faced lounge lizard distracted me with his barking, pissing on the gyre of a passing car my father was driving. I was impressed by the passion, the dexterity, the steady stream. As usual, Miss Edelstein from the evacuation centre was riding shotgun, giving directions between sips of a poorly-timed sundowner. It was all pretty much as expected except the saratoga tending a trolley of newborns in the corner.

After the circus

What sun will set here? Over sweet-wrappers
and ticket stubs littering back-lots where they
upped stumps, over ground compacted by slavish
tread—there and back, and back and here—over
the absent feet of jeering laughing lost souls
looking for a brighter boisterous light, not this
incomplete darkness, this half-light, evenfall,
where you trip over a tent peg and the fat clerk of
your big toe turns black with morning. Lingering
amid the fairy lights' candied glow hoisted on
shooting galleries, absorbed by laughing clowns,
blind heads turning this way to that, you watch
noisome crowds, a-bye, long down gone, diminish
and appear. Mercilessly their hands feed the
clowns, eyes on the main bet, the big prize stuffed
with cotton waste, the mechanics secreted away
under chipped paint colourful as the skin on
the strongman's arms where an anchor drops
into tides rising and falling muscled below. You,
slovenly kin of the carnival, watcher, gaper,
groper, stay-at-home, malingerer, do you feel the
slow snarl of dismay, listening to the organ grind
out promises off-key, the tune familiar, the script
effortless, while you jump about getting your two
bobs' worth? Beneath thick canvas, mesmerised
by tumblers and contortionists, by the mad

jumping monkey dressed as Napoleon riding
a mule's back, you listen to the three-fingered
violinist fumble notes, a crippled crab scuttled
on her fingerboard burst with music, hollowed
and thrown out. You touch the hilt the sword-
swallower offers and feel heartbeat on steel slid
cleanly from throat to chest. Needlessly you feel
closer, as your muted and caged dreams pound
away. The retinue seems endless, well-tried,
clowns falling out of the car's doors, the boot, a
restless hilarity, dashing the front rows in buckets
of confetti and water, fire jumping from the tip of
a finger into air, juggled amid knives, noise and
dark. The bearded lady sings an aria, a rake of a
man walks over broken glass, suspends a dwarf
from his testicles on chains made of silk, another
slips skewers through cheek and tongue, his eyes
zeroed into a horizon. You watch sequined tops
stuffed with breasts, feathers tickling so that the
crowd gasps, wheezes and guffaws but you hold
your breath, waiting for the truth of it to sink
in. Later, huddled between trailers, your drunk
tongue forces its way between words. The Chinese
fortune-teller's wet lips part, and you're left to
draw on prophecies in the strange language of
your future. Behind it all the generator's whirr

and clatter and the crowd, laughing, belching,
heaving up clouds of sticky sweetness and
smoke, sweat pouring out of light, and the sun
rising slowly over the now-empty lot where each
thing remembered slips away except the ring-
master's crooked beak, roman angles strung out
in limelight, and the steady gaze of the knife-
thrower suspended in the mid-air of afterward,
a dim forgetting you press against as you trundle
broken-toed up the road.

Any place to go

Days later, not long after we left the convent, the war ended. I promised to take Georgia direct to the train, but the sight of her on the back seat scrambling out of that uniform, and the highway opening up, well, what can I say but we're all sinners at heart. Neither of us had any place to go and when I made my suggestion, she crossed herself one last time, and wiggled her toes. We met Rodney outside Oodnadatta, holding the big red by the scruff of its neck. I told him, 'The butt of your cigarette is a refugee crossing to safety on your tired lips' tide.' He didn't care for pleasantries, so we set about the job at hand. Once the roo was staked out, Georgia and I jumped back in the Holden. I watched them disappear in the rear-view, like a movie's final scene as the credits roll. Rodney nursed the roo's head, whispering softly into her nervous twitching ears. When Georgia flicked the radio on and heard the ceasefire had broken, you couldn't blame her or feel too bad about Rodney and his frisky sweetheart. I told her, 'The world is a song left out in the rain.' She countered, 'It is ash daydreaming its fire.' I liked the drama of it, but preferred the way the flesh of her lips clung briefly together before she spoke, like loved ones embracing and going off to war. I forget the details, but remember the astonished faces driving past us, awkwardly mounted on the highway's curb, Georgia's sweet paddles waving out the window, her curled toes tangling cloudless blue.

Those ox-heart tomatoes

I told my son to clear the table. 'Jumbo,' I
said, 'clear that table!' I said it boldly just like
a father would. All the while he looked at me
askance, slowly picking up plates and the relics of
breakfast, orange peels and anchovy paste. 'Next
month, it will be the last days of February,' I told
him, benign with enthusiasm, 'Then what will we
do?' He was already at the sink, contemplating
the direction water flew down its plughole.
'We'll never be free of each other,' he suggested,
absently scratching the side of his head with a
fork. 'I expect we will wait for Mother's return
from Ryde. She'll bring us rich ox-heart tomatoes
we can scorch over the cooker's open flame and
eat on thick slices of bread.' 'If there's enough
gas,' he added, his thumb scraping fish-paste
from the butter-knife. 'Yes, with enough gas.
She'll bring us promises of church bells drowning
out morning.' 'We'll forget about the freeway?'
'Most probably we'll end up living in an ox-drawn
cart on beds of hay. We'll climb salmon ladders,
and eat their fresh pink flesh.' 'You don't know
what you're talking about, do you?' 'Well, at
least we'll forget the freeway.' I watched Jumbo
dry the plates, while I rocked back on my chair.
'Tomorrow,' I said, 'I will train the ox to hum

a concerto. What would you like? Beethoven? Tchaik? Satie?' Jumbo's disdain was palpable, noting 'Satie didn't write concertos,' flicking the tea-towel over his shoulder. 'Tchaikovsky it is then!' Even I knew my enthusiasm had grown a little strained. He put the plates back on the hardwood shelf and dropped the peels into the compost. 'It's almost a year,' he said wearily, sighing like a tube of paste completely squished out. All I could do was keep my mind on the bullocky and those juicy tomatoes she'd be bringing home, while the freeway hummed murderously by the door.

Wasted resources

Noah was desperate for a small advance. His new project, The Reinvention of Gills, was up and running, but he had to pay off the Harbour Authority to get the port flooded and the tunnels bricked in. Noah sent me a picture of the troublemaker Hartog, his 'moneygrubbing nemesis'. He was sitting on a settee in a dressing gown, an arm lazily draped over the shoulders of a tall blonde called Thelma. There was something domestic and licentious about it, like his-and-hers hand-towels at a swingers' party. In the background, behind the patio and the pool, you could just make out a sweatshop, the haggard faces of refugees battened down to work. Noah described it as 'some hidden agenda he was keen to reveal, a kind of ethos.' I knew it was a marriage portrait taken by a professional. On the back Noah had written at length about neo-conservatism, misogyny, the hideous implications, the infamy, about capital. I'm a sucker for daydreams and imponderables like this. I didn't understand Noah's jealousy though. I wondered if he truly loved Thelma and thought his empty promises would bring her back. Perhaps his whole project was a hoax, years of wasted resources, all that gene-splicing, DNA hacking, all the transgenetic razzle-dazzle, just a dirty trick to win over an old lover. I knew I'd never see the money again but I sent it. He'd never win her heart with his foolish schemes or free himself from the miseries of nostalgia. Hartog was too cunning for that, his research was well advanced. Poor Noah was all heart and ambition. As I sealed the envelope, Thelma swam about, slipping in and out of the water. Hartog talked on about profit margins and climate change. I sipped my Mojito, transfixed by Thelma's gorgeous brown neck, the gentle undulations of her gills, the unearthly way she would modulate from song to laughter.

Right people for the job

When my uncle got back from Burma, it was sixty years since anyone had seen him and he didn't look a day older. Ever since they were children, Mum always said he'd been the thoughtless type, always eating the last biscuit, or breaking her toys in his enthusiasm to see why they worked. 'He was a klutz and a dreamer,' she sniffed. 'Not a bad bone in his body, but not a thought either.' Once he lost her at the petting zoo of the Royal Easter Show. He drifted off in a simpleton's grin among the piglets and lambs. Somehow he reached Springwood before realizing she wasn't with him. She still remembers the scolding he copped from Gran, and the startled expression he wore days later, unable to unriddle cause from effect. Then, at twenty-two, he disappeared. Now Mum is in a home and upset all over again, crying into her floral nightie. She's aged ten years for every one of his. She can't understand him reappearing like that, surprised to hear about Pop and that slut of a waitress, or Gran and the kids she adopted at sixty, as the borders finally closed. He spent two days in the spare room leafing through family albums, the lost generations: his kid sister studying in an old shipping chest; the trip to China as a nurse; Dad revving up the driveway in an MG; their wedding—the last photos Pop appears in; Gran reading Henny Penny to Jack on the veranda; me in pigtails at six, pregnant at twenty-three; Jack on a trawler in the Gulf, turning to leather in the sun; Dad nursing my kids; Janey and Joe growing up in turn; Joe joining up at eighteen; Janey meeting Tong; little Nu dancing under the sprinklers on the front lawn last summer. After the third day entranced, shaking his big goofy head and pulling that no-nothing grin, he was gone. On a shopping list I'd left in the kitchen, he scribbled, 'We'll never surrender, love Theo.' But he's wrong. We'll get him this time. It's all in motion. We've laid down plans, contacted the authorities. We've got the right people for the job.

Lost soldier

The river was filled with bones from the neighbourhood's family pets. All sorts of bones: dog, cat, mouse. There was even the dusty rib cage of Mr Perkins, that old nag the Irish twins saved from the knackery and kept in their lounge room on the tenth floor. They used to bring Mr Perkins down in the lift and ride him along Seven Mile Beach. No one remembers when the bones started to collect. Some say it was after the last rains. No one can remember when they were either. Sometimes it almost seems ridiculous that water could fall from the sky. Mavis, the town's one-time spinster, claims to have the last wet season on video, but Joey found out that was just a lure. One afternoon, we pushed that dingbat Timmy down the bank into the bones. You could hear his big clumsy feet cracking like fireworks as a white cloud drifted up wherever he went shrieking about. He came back with the twisted vertebrae of some long lost and loved monstrosity. It reminded me of a book I'd read, how during some war somewhere they interrogated prisoners by skinning them alive. That riverbank made me think there was a lost soldier in town looking for some answers. I figure he lived under Brodie's place, in the basement where Brodie's Mum kept the dressmaker's doll and the family photos of the kid that went missing.

No second chances

'I burnt every bridge I ever walked across,' he mumbled through thick whiskers into his coffee. It was the morning the hostages walked back into the station, unharmed after a year in the headlines. 'I never asked for a second chance, and never gave any. I'm a man of this world. I don't harbour grudges or regrets. I don't know a thing about unrequited love, bad investments, long-lost friends or tax audits.' He was on a roll, you could smell the cinders of those bridges in his gravelly voice. 'I'm a self-made man. I left home at fifteen, and never looked back. I never knew a family except these two boots. I've been welcomed into every house a stranger and left so. I know the names of every street in every capital you care to mention. I don't have a mother tongue, each tongue holds me equally to its tit. I've broken bread with the poor and lame, as with the rich and mighty, and never changed, or looked back, or wondered why, or how, or when. I sleep easily, deeply, without dreams, without memory. I've never been depressed, or anxious, or fearful of any person, place or thing, but known them all. I've never felt fatigue, felt cold, or been wasted by heat. I've never given a second thought to success, fame, money, nor heaven and hell, or a life hereafter. They are empty as love, hope, trust, fate, or regret. I know the shape of my hands, the weight of my feet treading the earth. I know of no home to return to, I have no brother to call my own, no lover's warmth waits for me, or hearth beckons. I know what it is to kill and be killed, to travel without heritage or inheritance. I have held a bloodied stone in my fist and learnt what it is to exist.' His confession left me a little haggard and confused, as though I'd been dangled over the edge of a pitch black canyon, simply because I was in earshot. Gaunt smiling faces flickered across the TV screen over the bar, as he paid me five dollars for the coffee and started to exit through the side door. He turned as if on the edge of some further uncalled-for confession. I expected apocalypse, rapture, the ageless war, or to hear more of the brother he has killed over millennia. But no, not a word, not even a lousy tip, from that good-for-nothing, that cheapskate munted ape.

Symbiosis

He's speaking with his mouth full again, so it's hard to understand what's being said. This time sparrows are flitting in and out of his big trap, like his head was a chipboard bird-box. But he doesn't seem to notice or mind. It makes me think of flies gathering on an eyelid back of Bourke, of glaucoma. Anyway, he's talking about this and rambling about that, and all the while sparrows are hunting about on the table for crumbs, or popping their heads out from between his tombstone teeth to check what the weather's doing, or they'll balance for a moment on his tongue, which is fluttering away like a flag in a strong wind, and they don't seem bothered by all the movement and commotion, running about their little sparrow routines. He's going on and on about something that's not nearly as interesting as the little birds that have set up shop in his mouth for some god-only-knows reason. Perhaps they've developed a sort of symbiotic relationship, their own little ecology, a secret pact, or one of those living systems everyone's so worked up about. Whatever the story is, he's more interesting now than he used to be, when I understood his endless yabbering. These days, I slap his back with boundless love, shouting, 'Birdbrain! You've got it right all over again!' or smack a big kiss on his forehead, yelling, 'You sweet fool, Dingaling, we forged it, the winning ticket!' and dance a bliss-ridden rumba to the louche lines of the crickets thumping in my eardrums.

Compass

They wheeled me into the last room at the end of the corridor and there she was. It was happening all over again, just like Jorge said, '...again and again and again.' He was so tiring to listen to. He never had much of a sense of fun. Georgia told me it was because he'd grown up in a house without mirrors and as a child had no one to talk to. Even his imaginary friend left him. She asked, 'Can you see how different it might have been if someone had offered him one, even a broken one?' I didn't know if she meant a mirror or a friend, but either way, I wasn't convinced. He'd always been a bit of a galoot and a loner. I tried to imagine him at fifteen in a long hallway pulling faces in front of a mirror, light sliding off its beveled edges this way and that. In the background, church bells were ringing, though it wasn't the moment for spring mornings in high mountain passes or swathes of honeying light in the valley below. He had the anemic trace of a moustache on his lip as he puckered and pouted, his eyebrows dancing about at cross-purposes. When I tapped him on the shoulder he turned and there and then offered me one of the stones from his pockets. It had an arrow drawn on it in lead white house paint, marked in a child's hand.

It felt good and solid in my palm, like we had been one and the same many lifetimes before and might be so even now. He said, 'It's your compass. It will always show you the way there.' All these years later, I still marvel at it and can feel its weight deep in my pocket with all the others. I haven't needed to look at it in years, I know it led me here, that if I take it out now, it will be pointing to this room, this bed and the calm and loving face that has been waiting all along.

The Milonguero

Eventually we were a little embarrassed by Charlie Loquat's name, which sounded like something pickled in Chengdu and not quite suited to our particular desert, where at the age of forty-three he had chosen to live, packing up the remnants of his bicycle repair and tango consultancy and heading beyond the black stump to us. When he arrived in town, I was the first who sought him out. It was in my nature. I'd sought out others before and with some success. Old Mr Lees was the first, back in the autumn of '03, which harbinged much of what was to follow, Mavis and the Kenneally twins, Old Tom Lonely and Brother Drayford Dye. I've sought them all out at one time or another, but Mr Loquat eluded me with his shuffling gait and laconic stutter. In the end I only saw him the once, with Mavis, executing an abrazo at the end of Main Street before shuffling off on his bicycle. Mavis was never quite the same after that, none of us were. We all felt diminished. The Kenneally twins say he'll be back, they've seen it in a dream they built out of horse glue, some piping and slippers. Sure enough when they showed it to me, I knew they were right, that we'd have to be careful, that there was probably not time enough to master the necessary moves, to jerry-rig the town's fragile economy and rewrite the charter.

Lucky stars

It was a dry, cold night, perfect for sipping red wine. Jane Jane Edelstein brought me an orange juice and I thought about my lucky stars and all that dead light streaming down on us. Then she said nonchalantly, 'It's a dry, cold night, perfect for sipping red wine.' The word 'perspicacity' came slowly to mind, like light from those stars dying their tiny pinprick deaths, but I hadn't a clue what to do with it. The symmetry was almost perfect, but not nearly as good as Jane Jane's hips swaying over to the sideboard to get at a bottle of red. For some reason, I started thinking about flakes of sediment at the bottom of an empty glass and drowsy comforts. Jane Jane drew the cork out with a muffled pop, and I could hear the wine sucking in air, anticipating the warmth of our tongues and gullets. As she swayed back, glasses in one hand, bottle in the other, I guess we were both thinking, 'I've waited years for this.' Me and the wine that is, I've no idea what was going on in Jane Jane's head. Without a second thought, I was picturing droplets of wine splashed over her breasts, and my tongue stupid with them, guzzling every last drop. With the first sip, I briefly pondered the constellations teeming above us, but then she undid the first button of her blouse, and I was glad I didn't go for the orange juice or worry too much about those little pricks and their endless tinkering with fate.

Georgia talks to a painter

The way spirit tracks, in brushstrokes or words,
you'd have Buckley's of getting it right, sensing
how out here light does not fall. Waves of images
fill you so there's nothing but to paint, though
you don't like it, this country that's in you, the
red dust coating everything in one place or the
granite now, beneath your feet an island, quartz
and feldspar cooled beneath an ocean millions of
years departed before your arrival. The wattle an
edged blur in distance, melancholy of the sheoaks
weird, almost human with arms languorous,
supine to a brutality of light that in another
language might be what is. Gusts gathering yellow
sands, slow erosion, there is no foreground, no
back, harlequin mistletoe, cherry ballart, the rock
before you, holding light, sings like everything
else here, a silence you seek out the heart of.
So you work ten canvases at once though there's
no focal point, no cathedral to wash time across,
to track the changing planes of day, to assure
meaning, only what is built out of winds and dust
and rock and song now half-heard, half-dead,
unlearnt names scattered on a map. The idea
of elsewhere you leave behind or end up like
one of those figures in a landscape pointing the
way ahead, to something picturesque beyond

the frame, the perspective warped by some
new Eden, some ancient Arcadia waiting to be
plundered, a lie like the emptiness gathered and
named and transported here to build on. Your
eyes trace the scrub, manna gums and yellow
gums scrimshawing landscape, red gums sketch
out a vertical line like a man practicing his whole
life to say a single word, finding his bearings in
a place he can only come to slowly. Crossing the
lava, basalt, time uncovers you, uncovers land, an
aspect of light so what you abstract is not self, not
place, not moment but all these spoken by marks,
scars in a greater shared immensity, a flat dun
coloured space, a stillness where the delusions of
horizon have been erased, skins peeled back, as if
death could be cast off, its flesh left to dry in sun,
and time curved on itself, a husk. You watch in
tongues of light, listening with eyes, unearthing
spirit amongst boneseed and sundew, perhaps
love, in daubs of skyless light, learning country,
speaking it as it speaks you.

Cast away

You're a message in a bottle cast into the ocean forty years ago at the end of a great conflagration in a country no one cares much for anymore. Drifting in that ocean of yours, there are the great things to ponder: sky and ocean, and you between with the message you carry that no one has read. It's all so heartless in its ways, this mystery that was halfway through when you awoke. Even if you knew the beginning you doubt it'd make much sense and somehow know now the end will be a let down compared to the horrors you've been imagining in the quiet moments, which are many. Still, the sky is endless and the ocean deep and it's warm here inside the unnameable. When you drift back to the haste in which you were written, that long arc of inertia that sent you out into the breakers and the days heading out to open ocean, you feel a little teary with everything that's passed and the hope that started it all. Some nights, rocking on the waves under the stars, you remember being in pieces on the shore and her hand quickly scribbling you into being, the distant cracks of gunfire bursting distance, the night sky bright with burning buildings and those rough voices getting closer, when she stuffed you in your glass cell and sent you on your way. It's true you will never get out and so you're left to wonder what witness you bear: an accusation, a plea for mercy, a suicide note, perhaps a last ditch love letter.

Character actor

Where is this town Justice? Will you lead me
there? You're clawing at the eyes of a movie
poster, wanting a warm nook to sob in and me,
I'm a flat expanse staring back at you, mouth
firm and breasts insistent after all these years.
You wanted to watch yourself age in our faces,
but it's Dorian-Gray-in-reverse, and you're the
painting hidden away, the truth we're all afraid of
here. It's not the money or the inevitable causes,
the occasional, inconsequential double-binds—the
kids from Africa, the property in Dubai—it's you,
you're more of an abyss than Darfur. Your truly
bad teeth and, worse, the debt, the death that
takes a lifetime, none of it fits our dreams. Your
method's old, your character too variously flawed.

Trembling ontology

I'm in love with a dapper limber'n'limbic ladyboy
I met online who claims her name is Jesus. I love
the way she pronounces it and bounces me on
her knee. She makes me feel like a referendum
on family values in the posthuman age. I vote Yes
enthusiastically without a care for the phrasing,
the tricky syntax of the question. It does no
good, I'm disenfranchised and unregistered.
I have no kith nor ken to speak of. Her name is
probably not Jesus, and I'm not even sure she's
a he, or he's a she, or where the semantics end,
but she's holding onto me for now, convinced
we're a plausible narrative to play along with, a
passion play of sorts, a little obvious, but not too
flagrantly obscene.

Alibi considers the suburban line

My father was an accountant who became a suburban lawyer who dreamt he was an Alaskan bear hunter. Every day he would set off on the train at the same time. He'd take that old red rattler up to the city, repeating the names of the suburbs it passed day-in-day-out every day of his life. Sitting on the top deck, where the sun could warm his stubble, he threshed nets and snares and oiled his three-o-three to the chorus of passengers egging him on. When he got off at Central, he strode the pedestrian tunnel and on to the trailhead that curved its way to the mountainous bear country beyond. Once, I'm told, he took a wrong turn and spent days in the savannah, completely out of his depth. He came home sunburnt and shaken. He confirmed that lions sleep up to twenty-three hours a day, living only fleetingly in this world, with its bloodlusts and hungers. 'Beautiful animals,' he said. 'But, child, give me the deep wintry sleep of the great black bear and the long summers that follow.'

Hyde Park

In Hyde Park, she is foraging once again for a name. She walks up to the young couples and offers to trade their names for forecasts of distant cities. One in three accepts though the airports have long since closed. Cynthia, Stellar, Hardacher Jones. She pats the young girl's Chihuahua and feels its fervent desires gnawing away inside her. Buttonholing a jogger, she warrants, *Conlige suspectos semper habitos*, and feels a little better for it as he jogs off puffing, *sum, es, est, sumis, estis, sunt*, which recalls to her young James Edwards' neat cursive and big ears sitting next to her in the summer term of the eighth grade. For a moment she glimpses his eyes staring at her from the back of the jogger's head. It's touching the tricks memory has started to play on her. Hurriedly digging out names she'd stored for winter under a Moreton Bay Fig, she runs after him, pushing past the couples huddled together awaiting the tropical downpour that's started to descend not far north of Launceston.

Jumbo and the happy abyss

Now he's up there on stilts, hammer in hand,
tapping along the edge of the gutters, beside
the monstrosities he's been building, lover of
boundless misconceptions, my sweet father.
He says he's building a stairway, and sure
enough, he is, though I doubt it's one we'll ever
use. It stretches and strains into the sky above
the house, sways in the westerly breeze. He's
lucky summer is over and Alibi's away again in
remand. She'd have taken an axe to it and him
to task. He says weeks back, he saw her face up
there, a giant cumulous nimbus, and when he
went out and called to her, she rained down on
him, drenching him to the bone. He says it was
like it had always been, her kisses washing away
the months, easing the world from them. I told
him the world didn't care. She hadn't even been
forgotten. It was like she never existed. Even we
had replaced her with things we tried not to talk
about. I'd seen it looking out from him, and Alibi
and from friends. There it was again in the old
couple on the corner shop, peering out, quiet and
inquisitive, some ancient, animal thing. There
it was in the school kids' faces making a racket
as they passed the house home mid-afternoon,
happy in its element, a riot of sense open to it, the

autumnal bite on its numberless eyes. Maybe Dad is right. He has a thousand plans and blueprints. Maybe one of them will work. He's tottering on the edge of the roof, ripping up the copper guttering, the lead flashing and hammering it into his ladder, wavering two stories above the house. He's ripped up the roof-tiles and lays them out, each one a step, a little red chipped tongue, he tiptoes up. He's pulling himself up by his bootstraps. Impossible dancer. I wonder when the council will get here and tell him to pull it down, with their ordinance and physics and if he'll get finished before then, and clamber into the sky like he wants, to whisper to his cloud wife, to shout all that unsaid, and give her the kiss he's been lugging around like a corpse on his back, a weight that might yet take flight and bring her back or set him free.

Noah in love

'If one of us dies, I'm moving to Paris.' That's
how it started, love, liquid and light, no escape
clause, no pre-nup, a cardigan and fluffy slippers
and the refrain of per capita happiness indexed
against inflation. #2+2=5. LOL. It's a business
strategy, gimlet, not a song! We'd friended on
Facebook. I'd been distracted, cruising drunk,
hoping for just a little disambiguation, to be
fluently human as YouTube. Then the fateful
day she updated her status and a little part
of me died. I'd followed their relationship for
months, lurking on the edge, thrilled by the
singularity, of love posted, cascades intoxicating,
distant and sweet. I learnt French, then tried
my hand at Java, HTML, PHP, wanting to slip
under the skin of things, to get to grips with the
apparent devotion, the lack of context, the ease of
emotion. Think of it, *Wherever US is, WE are!!* I've
downloaded everything, I'm learning every move
she made on the *Boul'Mich'* late last summer. I'm a
study in readiness, the promise of reincarnation.

Team spirit

I was at the end of an unbearable drowsiness when the crowd erupted. It was like Pompeii all over again, semi-recumbent figures beckoning this way and that, and a man's head sticking out of a pile of ash giving directions. I'd been in the propaganda unit for years and had never seen anything like it, the sheer audacity, the uncalled-for chagrin. But I was wrong, Smythe put the order in. Little Prodo upstart, it's no wonder things were going from bad to useless on our side. 'No team spirit,' that's what the T-shirt had said, 'Sang froid!' At first I liked it like that: biblical, you're either with us or against us, an eye for eye, all of it. We'd put in sound-bites, pull out trumps. We talked up evil, liberators, freedom fighters. It was a rush, a contact high. But now? I should have listened, and never gone to Bondi. When we signed up all those years ago, I was just a simple monk of little faith tending spot fires, unemployed, anxious and angry, but he had visions, ambitions, drew things for us on the grand scale. Before the Great Forgetting set in, I'm sure I was happy and all this was different, but soon the money-lenders will be at the door again, and we don't even have a biscuit to bribe their baboons. Oh Lord, Lord, I'm so afraid.

Sidereal days

Every morning I hear it. The siren running smoothly up the street telling us everything is alright. I hear it coming from the distant suburbs, crossing over continents of sleep, following the spread of time layered in earth, light moving in certain fractions, mean solar seconds, to arrive reassuringly here. It seems consistent. Every day it says the same thing, in the same words, with the same insistency. Reliable and measured, consistent in its logic, the voice tells me every morning, 'It's going to be ok. It's going to be ok. It's going to be ok.' At first it was someone else's voice, a woman's, soft and official, adamant as a river stone, then it reminded me of my father's voice overheard from a distant room but meant for you. 'It's going to be ok. It's going to be ok. It's going to be ok.' Then it was her voice, a song it was easy to reawaken within, that sang through me over and again, each night and every morning the music fixed and present as the sun, numinous and eternal. But it didn't last. Now I hear the voice is my own, telling me, 'It's going to be ok. It's going to be ok. It's going to be ok.' Too insistent by half. Every morning, there it is again, my voice, somehow recorded and playing from the vans that glide effortlessly up the street, reassuring the whole neighbourhood. But it's all wrong, that's obvious. I've started staying up, waiting for its monologue, to start the day with a sense of the years passed, with the same modulations of welcome. But I know it's started to arrive a little early, a little late. It's unsure of itself, sometimes shy, sometimes brash. Just by seconds, a solar second here or there, but it's enough to undercut everything it claims. I'm keeping track of the precise times it starts over. I have instruments. I have tables. When the waves of sound reach me each morning and I'm measuring them against the position of the sun and the position of the stars, I'm starting to see what's going on, what it is I've been saying all along. It's going to be ok, I know that now, it is going to be ok. I'll be ready for them when they come with their charts and their frowns and the aching in their own hearts. I'll know what to say, I'll know what to tell them.

Monochord

One dog, one bull. I always said that sort of thing to myself. After all, one cannot be a self on one's own.

The man in the boat

Speak that I may see thee Ben Johnson, but that's right, you're risk-averse and, well, dead. It is a poor kin that has neither whore nor thief in it, so go de-spiv the mallee strife with a modern stump-jump plow for if truth is god's laughter you'll never win without a narrative. You're right, I'm stringing us along, waiting for some sense to it. How's this then: Long and thin goes too far in, short and thick does the trick. Mavis taught me that one right before the crash, but it wasn't just her simpleminded backstory. What mortal man can shed immortal guile, you ask. A fair cop. I was always slow on the uptake and meaning well. That's how it was in the naughties merging with machines. Go ahead, count to ten, it'll all be over quick sticks. No matter the banks have turned turtle and as frigid as when she drops off the kids. Every foot they grow, a metaphor for the years etc and so on and so forth and tra la la la lah. In the end, I gave up the fly-on-the-wall and the god-like view entirely, and shazaam, I'm here.

Authentic

I'm a quiet and generic soul trying too hard
to please. It's not authentic. I'm out of touch
with the habits of my group but predictive text
helps, its soothing tyranny. I spend the daylight
harvesting caresses from a lithe machinist, a
sinewy little clunker called Penny. Eventually
she will figure out I'm not a very good person,
so what's the point in hiding it, neither is she.
She's so depressingly empathetic she'd jump into
a mass grave if she could, and I might follow
her yet. There is no one to save us from these
microbes, the shuffling deck. So many points on
our horizon we could launch out from in the
random mutation we share. Onwards then, until
we find each other ready-made and to order.

Former lives

As I wheeled him out into the garden, the professor muttered how he'd once met Aristotle. He hadn't gone in for small talk the way that git Jesus did after a drink or two. They'd met on the seafront in Beirut during the 1980s. In retrospect, he thought they had both probably been spies, and were trading information. Or perhaps only he had been and that's why things between them never worked out. Back then anything seemed possible, he said, but now there were so few pricks to kick against. The rest of the evening passed quietly, set against a waxing moon and the vague scent of jasmine.

Margin call

First Thelma removed her pinky, then her left foot's five toes, little one last. Dutch quipped, 'The shoe's on the other foot now, sugar plum,' and we laughed in unison with the watching talking heads. Thelma kept her cool, her smile knowing and discreet, her scalpel wielding its economies. Dutch continued overplaying his hand. From there it went quickly, the cutting and the commentary until there wasn't much left you'd call Thelma, just a wrong-headed idea about volition, intention and the limiting of supply.

Growth cycle

When Old Tom walked out of the desert, the world seemed to be put aright. Jonas stopped his drinking and went back to working the Wind Farm, collecting and cleaning the battered lorikeets and rosellas, making a line of fascinators he sold at the school fete alongside the lamingtons and pikelets. Tom said little the first few months. The sun had damaged us all that last winter. I'd see him at the general store most nights, renting four or five DVDs, with a take-out Mexicana and a six-pack of beer. He grew fat and lethargic, started to fit right in. By late spring, he was back at the plant, working the evening shift, down in the hole, lugging and grunting and shuffling with the best of us. Things improved, back to the norm. Jonas rabbited on about fiscal easing, demand picking up, of a good third quarter, rumours of possible expansion. We never talked about it though, not directly, the things we had had to do.

Willful Blindness

'I wouldn't swap it,' Theo said, taking the tyre iron from me by the roadside. My head was a series of Swedish landscapes again, a flat horizon, leafless trees and the bite of cold. It had a way of skating off by itself when things got tough. If it wasn't slowly parting thighs, it was wilderness, with not much I could do about it. A road-train slammed past us in a cloud of red dust and gravel. I caught the grim faces of the truckie and the Aboriginal kid for half-a-second. Who knew where it all fitted together, it wasn't like the tourist brochures. 'I wouldn't swap it,' he repeated, the tyre now back on. I'm not sure either of us knew what 'it' was, let alone what might replace it. The little boat was off-balance as I climbed in and put the oars in the rowlocks. They held tight. Setting off in the thin arctic air, ice floes breaking across acres of empty sky on pale blue water.

Thelma seduced

By late afternoon the ape toyed with either eye
contact or The Gaze, hunting where the ducks
are and all that. None of it mattered: the quaint
hand-written notes swapped after going offline,
her casual spill of scent (almond and ammonia),
the differing terms of trade. She said the silence
of good people is worse than the actions of the
bad, which rang true as she drifted far from
focus, into a series of stats and predictions,
then those emaciated redundant faces asking in
perfect broken English, *Will we heal each other?*
Unlike contempt, most evils are easy. But even
contempt can be mastered. So he did another
line, gagged the slug and muttered, *Why heal
thyself, Adam Smith*. Then zeroed to her jeans' cleft,
wondered, *Another dirty gin martini?*

Sidekick

He grew increasingly interested in the walls, in their differing fates, and each day would approach one to ask what it held in and what it held out. They were a mute, defensive bunch for the most part, but beguiling in their ways, even coquettish at times, so he persisted, good-cop-bad-copping them with the loquacious summer sky, who for reasons of her own seemed hell bent on breaking them.

Unwilling

After the Great Forgetting, the city fell. All the political prisoners were released as no one knew who they were, let alone whose. The trade in organs and body parts abounded, not all of it unwilling. We picnicked around the ancient city walls, the contusion of history played easy with us, the joke of what it and we determined. Jonas winced a little, leaning forward to dab his bread in the hummus Mavis had brought, before returning to the parable of the retrovirus and the balance of trade.

Modern Odysseus

I was an anxious type who overthought tying their shoes. *Which personality disorder is characterised by elaborate personal fantasies and a complete lack of desire to maintain relationships?* It had been a long journey to the fridge, fraught with dangers and dilemmas, the unblinking violence of what it held terrified me. *Which personality disorder is characterised by feelings of inadequacy and extreme fear of being disliked or humiliated?* Thelma had said as much the day she left with the tradie named Wayne, who in another life might have been avuncular. *Which personality disorder is characterised by extreme mood changes, unstable relationships, and periods of dissociation?* Safe to say we were in this one, and he was just a balding schmuck she picked up at the local. *Which personality disorder is characterised by very strange thinking and behaviour along with uncommon beliefs?* They'd tied third in the Trivia night at the Blue Gum and split the meat tray. *Which personality disorder is characterised by extreme suspicion of others?* Talk about a euphemism. *Which personality disorder is characterised by a strong need for approval along with inappropriate seductive behavior?* I was probably at home waiting for the opening, the ringing of the bell, while he was ringing hers. *Which personality disorder is characterised by an extreme desire for order, perfection, and control?* I can still remember the cascade of figures, transnational desire trapped in an algorithm. *Which personality disorder is characterised by excessive thoughts of personal power, vanity, and image?* I'd get a bespoke suit, perhaps a TAG Heuer, and find some other lovely to blow my nose. *Which personality disorder is characterised by a pattern of disregard for and violation of the rights of others?* Marriage was the last thing on my mind. *Which personality disorder is characterised by an extreme dependence on others?* If not love then at least a certain economy.

The ape's second chance

'Everything in ruins, always and already, ever since we got the trick of our opposable thumbs.' That's how the ape put it, back again, for another round of stout and wasabi pine nuts, the hairy hipster Jesus freak. Since he last came round, he'd been to a spa to wash the fire and brimstone out and taken an MSc at LSE. 'Growth for growth's sake, it's in our DNA,' he hectored anyone in earshot. 'Ruins, ass scratchers, ruins, fathomless vistas of possibility, cleared and clean.' I admit, I was impressed, I'd never seen an ape in Zegna, and his girlfriend was a right little honey. She reminded me of Abandon, the one-time goddess of my one true religion, with all that fellating and mutual masturbation. Now there was a faith you could believe in! But he brought me back from my daydreaming, banging on the table. 'Creative destruction! Shock therapy! Everything is opportunity!' What was this old schlock they'd been teaching him, those ancient professors of the '50s. Dupe and a sucker, the perfect mark for a long con. I flicked the TV over the bar back on and the bodies were gone, unevenly counted then swept away into someone else's history. We watched the pointy heads and wonks reeling, sovereign debt etched across their foreheads, light pink hankies folded in Cagneys and Coopers. 'Swings and roundabouts, baby. Up or down, it's all the same to me. If it's broke, why fix it? Profit! I'm not the enemy. In this climate, we can all make a killing.' It was unclear who he was talking to, slathering away like a prophet, one hand on the honey, the other on the inside of his outstretched thigh. It went on and on like that for most the night. Eventually others came to listen, in twos and threes. He had a good point though that there'd always be the poor and it would be too slow to beat them up one at a time.

Coast roads

Nipples hard as bullets, that's how her way with words put it. There wasn't much left to say after that, with the ferry leaving at four. Given good traffic, I'd be home in time for the coup. I'd been holidaying, fixing fishing nets up and down the coast. I always had a gift for such things, prone to long silences and spitting the dummy. It's hard to leave new friends, but who could complain if the conversation soured a little between talk of pet hates and hobbies. It's true, like everyone, I enjoy the sound of a kneecap snapping. Am I criminal simply for saying so? Regardless, Jane Jane ironed the lapels of my uniform, made sure the gold braid sat straight, that the medals shone bright, appropriate given the circumstances. You have to love the attention to detail, her eyes always on the big picture. Driving up the coast road, with smoke gathering on the horizon, I still wasn't sure what her way with words was, but she always had plenty in need of fixing and you can't complain about that. I'm often staggered by the waste and carelessness of people, but I was happy to be on my way home, with countless heads ahead to crack, and those hard nipples safely tucked away.

A philosophy of freedom

The Dutchman came by. I was a little suspicious. Those scars on his face articulated a counter-intuitive femininity and got me thinking *Our best days behind us and only ruin ahead* is a philosophy of freedom for some. Then again, everyone has to trust somebody sometime. He handed me the tin with the attached string and I took the call. Sure enough it was old Hank Jenkins back from the dead, speaking in long quiet waves of kindness ill-suited to this world. Inside me the kid started up again, bleating in terror. I just listened and absorbed it, an impartial observer, an adjustment in the system. It wasn't until a few days later, in a different hotel, with the Dutchman's head wrapped in a towel and the gore cleaned from the tub, I was sure I'd made the right move, not following the Dutchman's advice nor that piece of string to its ineluctable end.

Born again bonobo

The warning came over the radio. *Fifteen percent off newborns, tomorrow only.* We wondered at that, what we'd show for it by Friday. But we'd been sidetracked. It seemed Noah was not all spot transactions and derivatives and might still have had his day. Perhaps come Friday, he'd be screwed like the rest of us, but for now he was leveraged and lubricated, ready-to-go. I demurred in the end, and let them have my fillings. It felt like my game face had been pinched and puckered by the invisible thumb and forefinger of a snotty-nosed five-year old God still getting the hang of things. Unfortunately, we were in need of some old-fashioned saving. The brokers knew it, with their makeshift stalls and winning smiles, the cheeky little chimp they hired to crank an organ on George Street, blowing bubbles. Georgia had got it wrong with her optimism and her convincing knitted string bikini. I'd gone along for the ride licking my lips with Abandon, the runaway bonobo we'd built a religion around all those years ago by the Yarra but by Thursday morning we were reassembling the newborns bought on the sly from Hartog, trying hard not to think about Friday and what was coming next.

MDPV

Old Tom Lonely copped it in a planking accident,
the tumble into politics and celebrity. A complete
cluster fuck. Who knew pathos still had currency?
But still there he is now, goofball autocrat
pumped up on daily fistfuls, nootropics and the
return of the startup. His minders shuffle him
away, lead him along on that ridiculous social
networking leash. Someone should tell them,
he's a meat machine like you and me. Lucid
dreaming, a hallucination, a trick. We're vehicles
no one's driving, so what's the point freaking out
or getting all lyrical. Soon enough, you'll wake
with something you might have said caught in
your throat and the sense of someone standing
behind you, watching.

Economy

When I awoke, Brodie was still there. He'd turned up a few days before, a week at most, with his button-down collar, starched shirt and side-part. He spoke softly and at first I'd found that comforting, though he never told me what he was in for, just that he was. That's all he'd say each day, in his gravelly growl turned low, 'I'm here now. I'm here now. I'm here now,' straightening his cuffs for emphasis, flicking some invisible fluff from his sleeve like judgment. Initially, I hung on his every word, offering whatever I had, the old love letters my mother sent from Borneo, the head-hunter's machete she'd brought back, my wife's engagement ring, my kids' first forays into foot and finger painting, that month's alimony cheques and the next's. He took it all willingly and never changed his tune. For the first four days of the visit I hadn't slept, caught up in the votive offerings, entranced by the wonderous things foretold, but finally my body gave out and I crumpled into bed. When I awoke, I was afraid it might have been a dream, but no, there he was, sitting patiently at the end of the bed, counting the notches on the hilt of Mum's South Pacific souvenir, murmuring like conscience, 'I'm here now. I'm here…'

The monkey-headed god of a thousand faces

For two nights in a row I walked down Pitt Street
in a T-shirt and nothing else, my tackle blowing
in the wind as Jenkins noted in the police report.
It was a little embarrassing, like blurting out
something you don't learn the meaning of until
later. I'd always been the careful type, counting
syllables, working against sentimentality, wearing
overalls to bed. Obviously things had changed.
When I went looking for an excuse, I realised
I hadn't been dreaming at all and those leering
bystanders really were laughing, not at me or
my tackle or my rampant lack of clothing, but
what they saw beside me, a monkey-headed god
of a thousand faces. Each one was chattering to
the other, telling its secrets and when I listened
closely I too started to laugh hysterically and edge
off sideways. I don't know how long he'd been
there or where he was going. It was so frightening
and familiar, it made my naked genitals seem
apologetic, humble, trivial to say the least.
I wondered when he'd escaped the petting zoo
and what he'd planned for later that afternoon.

Aimless

I drifted out far beyond ill-reputed water
metaphors, tipped off by a cunning editor.
Careful not to turn oceans to sand I considered
cityscapes as the inside of a river oyster. I gave
up amphetamines and yoga hunting around for
an autobiography I could live with. I ate hearty
steaks and wandered aimlessly, willingly, until
blind chance knocked at my door yelling, 'The
Gold Coast saved me.' I saw everywhere I'd gone
wrong running about in her hazel sun-filled eyes.

World already

The world was already the world and we
were looking for ourselves. Like something
mispronounced, we kept repeating our names,
each syllable a slice of concrete we tied to our feet
for security. In those days, there were stories, an
uncle ascending into cirrus, an aunt who never
surfaced again, we dreamt of the long narrow
road, the precision of a snowflake falling, the
wrong turn that always got us there. In the end
we went out beyond the scrub, to the free-to-
air stations, thinking about sophisticated things,
branch stacking and pork-barreling, the light
in her smile or the time in the middle of an
interview she reached out and touched his hand.

Thelma and the ape

Hayek, my slippery eel, tell me again about
the cake and the treacle. I can hear your calves
fattening under the table, but don't let it worry
you, you're still sexy as a tollway, my sallow
schadenfreude snookie. Here, take my hand and
lick my tongue, tell me again about your second
cousin Ludwig and how your great great niece is
Selma. Why, you're having me on, all that sounds
like a metaphor. It's true, your moustache has
become a hint sinister, but let's not dwell on that.
Ernst Macht set you free, right? Your nose knows
a thing or two about this upsy-downsy sensory
disorder we're disentangling. True enough,
you could sniff out a buck and wanted to call it
freedom. Come back to the couch that's appeared
in the corner just for us to snuggle on. Mime to
me again the sound of the last cable car on the
Loop and all those faces peering out, haunting
you in the dark.

Human, perhaps

You've arrived at the border, briefcase in hand,
bowler hat on head, peering patiently over the
jagged line someone etched out in permanent
marker. The border guards are muttering
in dialect. A street vendor weighs freshly cut
durian. A stray dog licks his balls and stretches
out in the harsh November light. You peer again
at the mystery of the six pink nipples on the
mutt's serrated chest. You've been practicing the
gestures that make you just so, human, perhaps,
but below that, the animal body, muscle and
blood and bone and hunger and the calm and
forgetting surrounding it, the white noise warms
your eyes from inside and somewhere there it is,
the face you'll never see. Then the fat one starts
to yawn, and shortly, so will you. You know you're
not alone seeping into tomorrow. You tore up
your passport in the last town and they say your
eyes will be next.

Bolthole

Brodie too was moving forward until he came on the last Dalai Lama. Optimism meant a truce, sure, but Brodie was more a glass half-broken guy in the Sydney-style. A loving and open face, massively unknowing, the sweaty lure of the larrikin, with its promise of violence a little like sex. He was a bit player, but not unaware, not without his reasons, a certain degree of volition, nous enough to shape a scene, to reinterpret the shades of failure. Innocence done right could kill after all, much as every community wants a lamb to slaughter. The whole kerfuffle started over a mistranslation. Jonas, the translator, was a Davos washout, shell-shocked, disabused and borderline. After the kidnapping, he'd tortured them for days with his rhetoric. They say it was out of spite for his perfect grasp of deixis and the beguiling lisp. When Hartog eventually tracked them down to a little shack on Google Earth, Brodie and the translator were so traumatised, so brutalised and beaten, it was impossible to tell them apart. After that, everything just sort of fell into place, with plenty of blessings all round and no lack of karmic banging on about the diminishing returns.

Millenarian conga line

The police pepper-sprayed each other in a show of strength, rounding up random bankers and brokers to comment on the fractals of the thin blue line they'd conjured. They cooed and purred fiscal responsibility as they dusted off and lubed their long-forgotten night sticks, which still knew a thing or two about taking a beating. By bedtime, I was walking down a forest path in a penthouse at the W, holding onto the stump of a woman called Gunter. She explained how her father had always wanted a German, noting, 'You see, the inconvenience of missing one hand, is generally outweighed by always knowing what the other is doing.' I didn't though, see, my eyes still stinging from the afternoon's fun. Without her, I expect I'd still be a seventeenth-century cobbler eating loaf upon loaf of black rye bread, endlessly slapping my buxom wife's generously-proportioned buttocks.

Autoethnographic

And still the feeling hadn't left us, something had been missing all the while, back there, beyond the Great Forgetting. Worse, the moments when we could convince each other it wasn't not there had become fewer and further between, a daily clutch of episodes before that great ocean of mind would slink in, crueling. It was a junkyard, a shipwreck, a six car pile-up at the tip of our tongues, perfectly out of reach. Georgia suggested we were characters in a pilot for a TV series that never went to air. Someone had been picking us off one-by-one since the last ad break, taking the weakest, the meanderer at the back of the pack, the sweaty little accountant with the pocket-protector and broken glasses, the cheerleader in matching Adidas skirt and mules. There had been a series of pits, balled spikes, bear traps, bodiless hands reaching from the brush, faces concealed in sweat-stained hoodies looming out of the damp forest that was otherwise so distractingly scenic and exploitable. At night we could hear the muffled breathing nearby, a hunter's soft tread, voices turned low plotting in a language all their own. We were in a forest of cannibals, overrun by human sacrifice, suicide bombers, terrorists, sub-prime mortgages and hoodlum cross-dressing freaks. Each morning we took a head count and the two of us were still there, while the day stretched on repetitive and overfull with promise. The coast was just beyond the next rise, we would meet the friendly locals who would offer us the choice bits of their exotic cuisine and ancient folk wisdom, then validate our parking tickets before guiding us to the safety of a shopping mall. But Georgia was adamant, it was a cliffhanger we would never get to the end of. We were stranded, facing each other with only our fear.

Person of interest

It was not what I'd expected, when they invited me to the embassy. Obviously they had good intelligence for a nickel-and-tin dictatorship, so I thought I'd go along to see what else they had to pin on me. A small star apparently, the cultural attaché lurching from his greeting to jab it into my chest. He said, 'Listen quietly and you hear the universe expanding.' I could see he was a believer. Excusing myself, I made for the svelte twenty-something sitting alone at the buffet gobbling canapés by the fistful. 'Your hunger becomes you,' I said, roughly pushing three to five smoked salmon treats into her lilac maw. 'Would it be so unpleasant to gild a lily in the national interest, not least our own?' she muttered between mouthfuls. 'Charity starts at home,' I agreed, taking her hand, and running it through the foot long beard neither of us had commented on 'til then. She started to nibble gingerly on my whiskers, a school of tiny fish running through my corals. She cooed, 'The future is unfolding and next quarter, given a surplus, we can marry as destined in the foreign land of our childhood.' Over her shoulder the attaché paced between lewd and knowing glances. My handlers were shit out of luck. I'd walked right into the trap. Betrothed decades before in a little town by the Hawkesbury, it had all been heading here from the outset. No amount of Ms Edelstein's endless invention, her handy knack for quantum mechanics and exfil, would remedy the developing rationalism of our situation.

How I learned to stop worrying and to love the free market economy

We were always mucking about with the unmentionables trudging through the snow, winter closing around the heat concocted by our shared desires. It wasn't highbrow as we learnt to grind and crank our bodies, our saving grace, a phenomenology of cocaine cum commodities, the fires of hell these days reserved for the faint of heart and feckless.

Roughly-cut pages

Today I found somebody's lost youth tucked away in a book I bought from a goateed American called Chad. There it was set aside for a rainy day, sitting like a fat peach on a bed of rice-paper and forgotten promises. When you held it, it had an unearthly weight, and your face peered back, all fish-eyed and reversed, like being reflected up close on the lens of a lover's eye. Looking closer, I saw four wildly drunken nights, one ending in a punch-up, one winning a meat tray and the other two all bent out of shape in the morning. It'd started to hum like a cat as I held it, deeply satisfied, a little fleshy two-stroke idling beneath soft fur. I saw a rainy night, and empty streets crowded over by apartments, lit up like Christmas. I saw light filtering into the high ceilings of a rented room, and felt the warmth of a bed. The thing was hotting up now, purring like a maniac, getting into this guy's lost youth. He was drinking with Hungarian mafia on backstreets, clubbing in an abandoned quarry, driving fast along a harbour front. I saw gambling debts, street scuffles, harsh words, and then a girl with long black hair who loved the sound of creaking wooden floorboards under her bare, exquisite feet. She was reading a book of roughly-

cut pages, eating slices of persimmon from the edge of a blade. My fingers started to tingle with the grain of a table I'd built from scratch, and my nose filled with the meals we scoffed there, the crashing wine glasses, the Latin music, the lascivious dancing that followed. There was a long walk in spring rain, an early morning drive to ocean, her hand lifting a shutter on Siberian tundra rolling ten thousand feet below, the sting of shore break in winter, and foreign music sung quietly, off-key, two floors below. The whole thing was about to take off, judging by the racket.
I flipped to the inside cover, to a name scrawled in a childlike hand, and grabbed the White Pages. After twenty minutes and three wrong numbers, this guy Brennan was on the line. I told him, a little breathlessly, 'I found the rest of your youth folded in a second-hand book I bought from a guy called Chad.' He took it all lightly, though even I knew by then, I was a lonely revved-up crank. 'There will always be Chads,' he laughed, stunning me a little with his kindness.
I raced on to the hardest question I ever asked: 'I was wondering if you want it back?' But he just thanked me. He wasn't the wistful type. 'Keep it,' he said. 'I'm done with all that,' adding, as if

to reassure me, 'My kid's playing fullback on Saturday. You enjoy it.' And he hung up with the force and dignity of a man who'd made all the right choices. I envied him that, sure, but I was in a fury now, rushing on to my future, with its creaky wooden floorboards and those naked dancing feet.

Alibi at the start of summer

In backwards, sea spray thinning ash as the
city turns from itself, the ocean that brought
it faces off a dying westerly, bushfire winds
clipping sprawled edges of suburbia where Alibi
Wednesday lets slip her need for understanding
of this kind or another. Jumbo miles away, caring
for their father. His monologues, engines for
survival spluttering to life in aftermath. Alibi
had been hoarding for years, out there, her
gathering hunger, half-hearted aching, heady
with glue-sniffing, the primitive clutching of boys,
gathering up accounts, instants of ingratitude,
the overall lack of graciousness, salt-laced crest
and crumble of bodies, waves mimicking freakish
winds and seasonal change, determining which
way illumination might shed. Fifteen years is
a lifetime. You could suffocate, taking it in too
deeply so she learnt to bark and hawk. She
feels like the city, backed up against the sea,
dusk cornered and for once turning around,
capering headlands, licking names as she twists
newspaper into curlicues of flame and presses
against stripped skin of eucalypts, scraggle ends
of underbrush and banksia dry and tindered,
translating the flickering unthought to daylight
flame, rough and immediate.

Last exit to human

Keep in mind a series of exits were Charlie Loquat's final words. I've been building exits ever since, wooden doorframes I string out along the coastline and run through in an endless game of tip with a sheepdog called Boxer. Boxer licks my face and Tag! It all starts over, the panting and fretting and escalating excitement of being IN! The surf pours through the exits and recedes again. I expect one day I'll get there and either Boxer or I will exit to ocean while the other stands waving farewell from the shore in long slow arcs against a greying sky, breath easing slowly after years of THE chase, not a touch of sadness to it. I wonder at the Dogman's silhouette in my dreams, standing there on his hind legs, a freak of evolution, thick shoulders and stumpy forearms and paws, how when he speaks in that low growl, it makes me feel more human.

In the garden

Alibi claims to remember being in Mum's womb, wondering if she should be born. As if she had a say in it. 'Sure, I could lay around all day, food on tap, it was warm and I never needed to shit or bathe or do the washing-up. Mormons couldn't come knocking or market researchers or relies bearing witness.' I suppose she was right, she'd had it good, better than we do now, with Mum gone and Dad off in the shed welding scraps of junk together day in and out. He says he's building a time machine for us and we'll go and visit Mum soon, but I don't know who he thinks he's kidding with all that talk of neutrinos and space-time quandaries. Every day I wind back the clocks in the house a little. I steal a minute here, thirty seconds there, sometimes five, ten are enough. I take them then and plant them in the backyard. In the evening I listen to them growing and at night they flower as I drink my tea on the back step. I listen to Dad in the shed with his frantic hammering and sawing that has lately grown so soothing. I know that eventually, one way or the other, we'll get back there and Mum will sit with me in the dark watching the years and hours we lost flowering together. She'll put her mug down and then lean over and peel

away my face where she will find earth and time
tangled, overgrown and grown rotten, and then
digging below that she'll pull out handfuls of light
and send it on its way.

Countless times

It was one of those crisp blue winter days, just before spring, the ones when you think your nose might snap right off your face. We were walking across a mountaintop. The early morning air was a sheet of glass we skated down to the city waiting below. Watching the sunrise she turned to me and said, 'It's so beautiful, it's like the beginning of the world.' A bird turned sharply in the breeze, twisting this way and that. 'But what about all those people beheaded in dusty rooms,' I asked, 'like we're in the middle of some new-fangled Dark Ages? Or those soldiers stalking city streets we'll never be brave enough to visit, and all the cracked-up, hateful troubles filling the world?' Even so, watching that sun rise over the city, catching gold on the fir trees bustling about the valley below, I saw what she meant. The bird danced about without a thought for us. 'How did we get here?' she asked. 'Aggressive foreign policy. Peak Oil. Big Brother. Big Business. The bitter, greedy few…I don't know,' I said, stumbling on a loose bit of shale, 'Marshall, Le May, LBJ, Truman, Reagan, Clinton, Bush, Obama … *liberté, égalité, fraternité*?' 'No, no,' she interrupted, 'I mean here, this place and now. I don't remember going up the mountain. I just remember an angry voice muttering in the dark, and this last half-hour walking down the track. Now that I think about it, I don't even remember the name of the mountain, or your name, or mine.' She sounded terrified. Looking around, it was true. I didn't know where we were either, or how we had got here. Everything was familiar, like we'd been here countless times before, but none of it had a name, not even me or her or the empty valley below. It was all monstrous and new. I held my hand to my face and cried like a child. 'There, there,' she reassured me, taking my other hand in hers and leading me on, 'We'll just have to name it, that's all.' I saw then that she was brave and relentless. Everything would be alright. We had thousands of years.

Insert blank page here

I am a matter of conjecture, not all my own.
When I start to feel a little annotated, I catch the
Inner Critic up the steep incline of my inhibitions,
to the viewing platform where, yet again, I may
not find the wherewithal. Even after zipping in
tight to the zoot suit I call Cleaver, and kissing
my loved ones adieu, I feel lightly grounded,
peering out into all that false hope and good
will. I'd like to note while my body behaves like
a general fiction, it is nevertheless susceptible
to disease and afflictions not least the canned
laughter that masks a certain tenderness. I should
like to have called it 'The Willing Embrace' or
'The Reduction!' but I lacked the insight, the
neat trick of irony, caught up in all this lyrical wet
work. If I slowly remove my shoes and the wind
shifts, things change a little for the better. I had
hoped for a blank space to leave others to fill, as
they do, forgetting themselves after a drink or
two. It's good to lend a hand now and then, to
give something back, to feel the rush of things
run across the face they said was all your own.

This project has been assisted by the Marten Bequest Travelling Scholarships and the Commonwealth Government through the Australia Council, its arts funding and advisory body.

Interlocutor

'Time is a hoax under my skin,' he said picking up the bottle opener for emphasis. Jerome was a plod and a hack, but I'd loved him all my life and wouldn't stop now. 'My skin is the hint of the air we become,' I retorted. 'And the earth, sky eater!' he corrected. 'The pilot working your feet has lost his union ticket.' 'My face is an affectation in blue minor, a singular twist.' 'And your RNA, a passport, its tongue worn lightly.' 'A sentimental and sensual unaccounted biodegradability.' 'Starburst, monkey skull, you can't price-fix the senses!' 'I am what I was after all.' 'To be, verb licker!' 'And from that, lovely hard-heart? Earth and shit and fire.' 'Earth and shit and fire,' I cackled back. 'A crackle of blue light in the tavern of our heads.' 'A spurt and spray in our fleshvat of chemicals.' 'Sixty-three trillion dollars!' 'Sixty-three!' 'Every one pinpointing you!' 'And the gallery catching good.' 'Like the charred and blackened baby.' 'Still squawking in my arms!' 'Was it always and everywhere the Age of Serotonin?' And so on and so forth, killing time, releasing it gently from the confusion of our skins.